SOCIAL MEDIA

THE GOOD, THE BAD & THE UGLY

ABDUL VASI

Also by Abdul Vasi

- Entrepreneurship Secrets - Beginner's Guide To Running A Successful Business
- Bitcoinpreneur: A Beginner's Guide To Bitcoin, And Everything You Need To Know To Start Investing
- Tranquility- Finding peace in a turbulent world

CONTENTS

INTRODUCTION

If somebody had told me 15 years ago that social media would become crucial in modern society, I would have simply laughed. But in fact, that prediction has become completely real. Social media has become one of the most crucial technologies in the world and it is evolving daily.

Modern society has become much too mechanical. Everyone is running after their own goals and working hard to achieve milestones in their lives. As a result, we are constantly growing apart from the people we love and care about. The concept of spending time with the people you love seems farfetched in this modern era since our packed schedule does not allow us to do so.

It is true that social media helps people in a lot of ways. It has provided us with a chance to connect with others and put our ideas out front. However, social media is not always for the good of the community; in fact, it has some terrifying consequences.

Despite the good it does for society, social media has become like a spider web which is entrapping millennials to a great extent. It is the reason why people are falling away from each other.

Social media has become the reason why most people fail to meet their deadlines and live like a machine without any hope or ambition of their own. Even if they have the ambition to do something with their lives, they are running out of time since most of it is being devoured by this beast called social media.

As I continued my research on social media, I started to realize that social media has a diabolical nature. On one hand, it was acting as a platform for people to express themselves freely and interact with each other. But on the other hand, it was making people lose self-confidence, waste time and become addicted to it.

What is the right way then? Do you need to just deactivate your accounts and live your life away from social media? This thought really plagued me for days.

Social media is highly appealing. It is not easy to overlook it and get busy with something else. I understood that pretty well. But how would you be able to control yourself?

The mission was simple: I wanted to help fellow human beings suffering from social media addiction without having any clue on how to get out of it. Thus, I decided to write this book.

In this modern age, people have become psychologically lazy, weak and somewhat sadistic. The abundance of social media has to be blamed greatly for this turn of human civilization. The behemoth of information that social media offers is restricting people from trying hard to achieve anything. They are feeding on this information without realizing its deep-rooted consequences.

Just as a lot of junk food can make you physically unfit, too much social media junk is very harmful to your mind.

This book is a very special one to me since it also talks about my personal problems with social media addiction. It details how I have overcome the addiction and restored my life to normal.

Reaching the age of forty, I have gained a lot of experiences. I have always wanted to help others, especially the youth of today, with the things that I have learned throughout my life. As a result, I believed it was my duty to enlighten everyone, and especially the youth of today, about the good as well as the perils of social media.

I have based all the concepts on thorough research so that you can understand everything clearly. Furthermore, I have added my personal experiences in every chapter so that you can relate to everything easily.

I would also like to thank my co-author Ms. Ankita Roy Choudhury for helping me write the book in the best possible way. She added to my research and helped me set the right tone for my book.

However, it wouldn't have been possible without my family. I would also like to thank my beautiful wife and my daughters who have inspired me throughout the process. Without them, I couldn't have realized my flaws and the extent of my addiction towards social media.

Life is beautiful and there is a lot every one of us can experience. There is no need for you to remain entrapped in the digital webs of social media. Use it to make your voice heard. Use social media to reunite with your lost friends.

But do not become so engrossed that you start losing your dreams, ambitions, real-life connections, time and above all, your touch with reality.

Social media is obviously a brilliant tool that serves a variety of purposes. But do not let it become the master of you. Be the master of yourself and live your life on your own terms.

That is exactly what this book stands for. It is about balancing life without being addicted to social media. You will learn the good, the bad and the ugly about social media. Above all, it will show you the tricks to balance your life.

So, make your journey through the pages and make sure you truly become the master of your social media.

THE GOOD: ADVANTAGES OF SOCIAL MEDIA

1

SOCIAL MEDIA: A NEW HORIZON FOR THE MARKETING OF YOUR COMPANY

"Social Media puts the 'public' into PR and the 'market' into marketing."

— **Chris Brogan,** president of New Marketing Labs

The social media storm is widespread all over the world and there is hardly any doubt about the impact it can create. And some individuals, such as bloggers, YouTubers, etc., as well as brands, have taken advantage of this opportunity to turn their brand into a million-dollar business. There is no denying the fact that *this is the era of social media marketing*!

While there is an ongoing debate on the usefulness of social media, we cannot deny that it provided marketing managers with a new horizon. Of course, social media may have some disadvantages on a personal level but when it comes to marketing and publicizing there is nothing that can match the efficiency that social media offers.

As I said, the development of social media has created new opportunities for companies to reach out to their clients in a far better way.

If you are a business owner or an entrepreneur, you must already know how crucial marketing is to the success of your company. Whether you have a brick-and-mortar store or a web-based business, unless you are reaching out to targeted customers and enlightening them about everything you are offering, you cannot achieve business growth and success. So, you can obviously understand how important marketing is for the success of your business.

In the past, companies used flyers, banners, leaflets, posters, and advertisements in print, television and radio to publicize their goods or services. Yet the efficiency of these methods was not beyond question, and those days are long gone. Nowadays, you can do everything with just a few clicks on social media pages.

The goal of marketing is to communicate with people and educate them about everything you are offering. In order to do that, you have to reach out to your target audience first and that too on a personal level. The aforementioned methods help to reach out but they often fail to create a lasting impact on the mind of the consumers.

The posters, flyers or other conventional tools of marketing can easily be overlooked by people. They can easily wash off from the mind. So, what can you do to gain an extra edge? Well, the answer is really very simple. You need to utilize social media.

With the internet becoming easily available and the development of smartphone technology, most people nowadays are connected with social media platforms in some way. They are using social media to share their thoughts or to connect with others. And that is something you can utilize to help your business grow.

You can use enticing posts or promote exciting deals through the intelligent use of social media platforms to lure them towards your company. Social media lets you have a clear understanding of what your customers want and help you shape your offers in such a way that they can easily create a lasting impact.

Furthermore, social media platforms offer tools and resources to effectively market your products or services. Every popular social media platform, including Facebook, Twitter and Instagram, offers business profiles for companies. You can create a social media page for your company, run different ad campaigns, make interesting posts and track the performance of your campaigns in order to gain the best results.

From a financial point of view, the budget that you need to run social media campaigns is obviously much lower than what you need to market your business with conventional marketing tools. You not only get efficient results but you also achieve value for your money with the help of social media marketing.

As I mentioned before, social media platforms also offer you the chance to track the performance of your marketing campaigns. They offer you a separate dashboard where you can view all the statistics of your ongoing campaign. It shows all the data with which you can understand how many people have seen your advertisement or posts.

Plus, it informs you about the rate of conversion, which gives you a vivid idea of the response that you are getting from your marketing campaign.

The intelligent technology that social media uses also helps you understand the reach of your posts and advertisements on a certain budget.

Furthermore, you will be able to modify your advertisements to appeal to certain regions or age groups to get the most efficient results. As a result, you will be able to give appropriate direction to your marketing efforts.

"Social Media can provide a conversational extension to a B2B company's nurturing programs. Social Media gives us the opportunity to humanize our communications and make our companies more approachable." — **Ardath Albee,** CEO of marketinginteractions.com, said this in one of his interactive sessions.

Marketing is obviously an important aspect of every company. Without proper marketing, it is not possible to gain a competitive edge on your business rivals and achieve your business goals. The rise of social media has made it possible for every organization to achieve new heights through appropriate marketing efforts.

But what do you need to do? How will it help you? There are a few questions such as these that need to be answered.

In this chapter I will help you understand everything as clearly as possible. As you go deeper into this chapter, you will understand how social media boosts the efficiency of your marketing efforts and why it is the future of marketing. I will also shed some light on the processes that you can follow to ace your social media marketing efforts, through real-life examples and experiences that I have had myself.

So, let's dive deeper into the next part of the chapter.

Social media humanizes communication:

Communication has always been considered the most crucial aspect of marketing by marketing gurus. Proper communication is the only way through which you can transmit your messages to your customers and lure them to whatever you are offering.

If you are a seasoned marketer then you might already know how difficult it is to actually communicate with your targeted customers, especially if you are using the conventional tools of marketing. However, social media enables us to overcome those barriers and communicate with the customers directly.

Marketing teams of most companies often become familiar with their customers on a very personal level. They wish them well on special occasions like birthdays, follow their social media profiles and build a healthy relationship with their customers.

This technique actually can work miracles for companies. It convinces the customers that they are important to the company. This will help you increase not only your sales but also your rate of customer retention. In other words, good communication helps to create a special bond between the company and the customers, which is the key to the success of the company.

Though these things may sound impractical, you can actually achieve this feat if you make proper use of social media. Social media helps you gather a lot of information about individuals. From the name, location and birthday to interests, likes and dislikes, you will have a clear picture of an individual if you thoroughly research their social media profile.

An intelligent marketer always takes advantage of this information. Once you have a clear idea of what your customers are like, you will be able to customize your deals and offers accordingly to garner their attention.

Now let's discuss how you can use the paid promotion facilities that social media offers to attract your customers. While paid promotions are highly essential and crucial to every marketer, you also need to attract organic followers to your social media page. An organic clientele is most loyal and that is a proven fact. And you can only attract organic followers through appropriate communication.

Without proper communication and regular interactions, you will not be able to build an organic base of followers.

Yet it is not a hard thing to do. As I mentioned before, social media humanizes communication. As a result, by only putting in a little effort you will be able to build a loyal clientele for your company.

Let me tell you my experience to help you understand clearly.

I have been an enthusiast of social media for growing my business since its inception. I was one of the first few entrepreneurs to create social media pages for my company. Somewhere deep down in my mind, I was always aware that one day social media will become the real "GOAT" of the marketing world.

But in those days, social media had not yet become a worldwide phenomenon. So, we used to rely more on other digital marketing tools like emails and SEO. Everything was going pretty well until one day I realized that our marketing campaigns were failing to create a profound impact on customers in the way they used to do.

It really confused me and I dived down to find the root cause of this problem. I was quite adamant about finding where we went wrong with our marketing efforts. After thorough market research and dozens of meetings with my marketing team, I realized that we had been neglecting one big aspect of digital marketing. Yes, we were not socially active as much as our business rivals were. And that was where the difference was being created.

As soon as I realized it, I completely immersed myself in understanding how social media was doing wonders for other companies in terms of marketing. The first thing that

I understood was the efficiency that social media offers in communicating with customers. Being in the industry for several years, I was well aware of the power of communication in marketing. So, I did not waste any more time and asked my marketing team to increase our social media presence.

As instructed, my marketing team created social media pages for our company and optimized them. They started interacting with customers by posting regular updates on our social media pages, starting Q&A sessions and running successful social media campaigns.

Within a few months, the results started to surface. We were doing great in accumulating new customers and creating a big customer base. Our sales had been improved and we were again at the top of our field.

So, you can understand how social media helps you communicate and how it helps you gain customers as well as retain your old customers.

"The most successful marketer becomes part of the lives of their followers. They follow back. They wish happy birthday. They handle problems their customers have with products or service. They grow their businesses and brands by involving themselves in their own communities." — **Marsha Collier,** a notable speaker and business author, excellently summarizes everything that I have said so far in her quote above.

Social media really helps you to achieve the impossible once you know how to use it properly.

Provide your customers what they really want:

If you have the talent and opportunity in this digital era, then don't hold back from opening up to the world. You have the freedom of choice!

One of the most famous success stories is of Orabrush. Dr. Bob Wagstaff, the founder of this innovative product, failed when he tried traditional ways of marketing his tongue cleaner. But things changed when he started to drop YouTube videos demonstrating his revolutionary tongue scraper. And boom!

He had hit the right chord and soon his once-failed business had more than $1.6 million sales. It seems he knew what his business needed and he orchestrated the videos to bring in sales.

See, social media really turned a flop business to a profitable one. Smart, right?

Social media allows you to know about individuals and their likes as well as dislikes if you really research their profile. And that is exactly the thing that you can use to your advantage to show your customers what they really want to see.

With proper research and hard work, you will be able to understand what an individual looks for in a company in your own niche. You can also refine your research with respect to geographic locations and age groups. This will help you modify your offers and deals so that they instantly become a successful marketing stunt for your company.

Plus, you can ask your customers for suggestions or hold

live sessions at your social media page to understand what they are expecting from you before you create new deals or offers for them.

"If you make customers unhappy in the physical world, they might each tell 6 friends. If you make customers unhappy on the Internet, they can each tell 6,000 friends." — **Jeff Bezos**, the CEO of Amazon, said this at a convention. It gives you a clear understanding of how powerful social media actually is.

If you are really looking to make your customers happy then you will have to provide them with what they actually want. And social media allows you to do that with utmost efficiency.

If you think you are fit to be a blogger or influencer, be one. Give it a try. If spending unlimited hours on social media brings in business for you, then showcase your talent, your business ideas to the world. But present it in a way that will leverage you as an individual as well as your company.

A well-known fact: social media is the birthplace of new age start-ups.

Is it really a new horizon to the world of marketing? I think you know the answer.

2

CONNECTING WITH PEOPLE: HOW SOCIAL MEDIA BRINGS YOU CLOSE TO OTHERS

"Smartphones and social media expand our universe. We can connect with others or collect information easier and faster than ever."

— **Daniel Goleman**, American author

Human beings are social creatures. We live in a society and thrive by forming connections with one another. That is how human civilization has advanced rapidly over the years. However, in modern times, it has become more difficult for us to form connections and interact with others.

Every one of us is always running behind in achieving our goals. We are trying to make the most out of a day by utilizing every single second to our advantage. Busy schedules and demanding times have turned human beings into work machines that function to achieve targets. As a result, we are falling away from each other since the schedule that we follow does not allow us to do otherwise.

Amid all the hassles of our daily life, social media has truly proven itself as salvation for humankind. It has allowed people to form new connections and regain old ones. It is truly a gift that we have been given by rapid technological advancement.

Though there are people who debate the consequences of social media and the direction of our world due to its influence, there is no doubt that social media has truly helped people live a better life by surrounding themselves with others.

Life is very uncertain. We often do not know what will happen in the future. But what really makes life beautiful is the people that we connect with and the memories that we create with them. Yet as we journey through the road of life, we often tend to lose people.

Whether it is a childhood friend or former colleague, there are people who come into our lives at certain points. And they also disappear in the obscurity of our minds just because we do not have the time to keep in touch with them. As we grow up and become more focused on our goals, we keep on losing connections. Thus, a day comes when every one of us seeks someone's company.

Social media was developed with this idea. The concept was to bring people closer and regain the connections that have been lost. With the internet becoming cheaper with every passing day and the development of smartphone technology, most people nowadays are using smartphones to utilize the internet.

As a result, most people are connected to social media in some form. It has opened different gateways for people to find their old friends and acquaintances while creating new ones at the same time.

One of the best things about social media is that it brings together diverse communities. It breaks social barriers and helps people develop bonds irrespective of their class, creed, nationality and race. It actually allows people to be more open-minded and welcoming. Most interestingly, social media also brings like-minded people together.

Social media has been a platform where you can actually share your thoughts, likes and dislikes with others. So, it helps others know you better and often forms new connections upon the basis of shared interests.

Social media provides you with different features in order to interact with others. You can obviously share updates, pictures and other media. You can inform others about your mood, opinions and thoughts. This can bring you closer to other individuals who share your thoughts and opinions which can ultimately spin into a lifelong friendship or bonding.

Social media platforms also offer a DM (direct messaging) feature which allows you to directly interact and communicate with the people you find interesting and vice versa. In other words, social media is this enormous meeting place for people that you can leverage for different purposes.

Now, what does that mean? Why did I say you can leverage it for different purposes? Though initially social media was developed to help people interact with each other, decades later it has become this powerful platform that is giving a voice to everyday people. It has become a platform where you can make your voice heard.

Social media has given people the power to change the world and put their opinions up front without hiding them in the closet. It has not remained just a tool for interacting. This platform has handed the power to you to bring about change by forming strong connections with others.

Whether you want to condemn a ghastly act or simply want your opinion heard on something, you can voice all your thoughts by using social media platforms as the medium.

"The great thing about social media was how it gave a voice to voiceless people." — Welsh journalist **Jon Ronson** beautifully summarized what I have said so far.

Use the platform in a way that will benefit people. A few days back, I came across a story that stunned me.

It was an inspiring story about how a woman raised more than $160,000 (more than Rs 11 crore) to support a homeless individual. This incident took place in 2017 in Philadelphia where a woman who ran out of gas was helped by a homeless man. As per her tweets, the homeless man had only $20 (around Rs 1400) left. And without giving a second thought, he bought the gas for the woman by using that $20. It was surely a big sacrifice for him to give his last dollars.

However, this touched the woman's heart so much that she began raising money for him through Gofundme.com and Twitter. She tweeted the whole incident and the man, Johnny Bobbitt Jr., became an overnight hero.

Well, if people have the intention of giving and utilizing social media for benefiting someone, then others will talk more about the advantages of social media and less about its disadvantages.

But how can that be possible? How does social media connect you with others? A lot of questions still may be floating on your mind. Let us explore the concepts in great depth and understand how social media actually helps you in real life.

Reconnecting to the good old days:

Of course, this is one of the foremost things that social media helps you out with. It helps you to get reconnected with people whom you have lost due to your busy schedule and loss of contact. It helps you reunite and stay in touch always.

At some point in life, every one of us has a friend or acquaintance who becomes almost a complete stranger. In most cases, it happens as we lose touch with them. We keep our focus on our goals and careers, and it becomes impossible to regularly communicate or meet with someone.

As a result, long before you realize it, you become a complete stranger to a person with whom you once shared a good friendship. And truly, this is the saddest part of our modern life. We do not have time. We are so busy running after our targets; we do not get time to do anything else. So, it is nothing unnatural to lose friends and acquaintances as we grow up.

Most important, you must always remember that the way you are chasing your goals, the other person is doing the same thing too.

Recent studies show that most people ages 16-60 use social media. So, you will have no problem finding the social media profiles of your old friends.

With the passage of time, social media platforms have become quite intelligent. So, if you know someone's name then you should have no trouble finding them. Furthermore, you will be able to modify the search to a certain locality to make the searching process much faster as well as efficient.

Once you find the friends you are looking for, you can follow them on social media, contact them through DMs and catch up on everything that has happened in the past years. Plus, you will not have to go the extra mile to maintain your connection and spend time with them.

Following their profiles and occasionally texting them from your smartphone using social media apps are all you need to keep in touch with your friends. And everything is possible with the help of social media.

My personal story will help you grasp the concept.

During my college days, I had a friend named Rakesh Kumar. We used to spend our time together and have fun all the time. From studying together to partying on the weekends to occasional long drives, we were truly best of friends; we were like brothers.

But everything changed soon enough after we finished

college. After graduation, I dedicated myself to developing my business. I worked day and night tirelessly to make my entrepreneurial venture successful.

On the other hand, Rakesh went to Germany to pursue an MBA. In those times, making international calls was a costly affair. And there were no Skype, IMO, WhatsApp or other video calling apps. So, keeping in touch with each other was very troublesome. For some time, we used to send each other postcards. The frequency reduced gradually as we both became very busy with our lives. Suddenly, it stopped one day. That was the last I heard from my best friend.

After a few years, I heard that he had married a German girl and had settled in Frankfurt. I was happy for him. But somewhere deep down, I would always miss my best friend.

My hard work paid off. I became a successful entrepreneur. Everything was great as I always planned it to be.

One day, I was going through my Facebook profile. Suddenly, I got a notification. Rakesh Kumar wants to be your friend. Yes, my old best friend had sent me a friend request on Facebook. All the memories flashed before my eyes instantly.

I went to his profile and checked his feed. I found that he had become a director of a reputed organization. I saw his photographs with his wife and two little boys.

His appearance had not changed much except for the moustache and French cut beard.

I accepted his friend request. Opened the Facebook messenger on my phone and sent a "Hi."

He replied, "Hey, dude! Long time no see."

And all of a sudden, I found myself chatting with him and catching up on the things we missed in all those years.

I was reunited with my best friend and I rejoiced. And I owed it all to Facebook.

I am really thankful that social media helped me get back a person who has always been very close to me. This is the power of social media. It helps you get back the people in your life.

"Social media is reducing social barriers. It connects people on the strength of human values, not identities." — **Narendra Modi,** the Indian prime minister, beautifully describes how powerful social media is.

What's wrong with exploring something? Building new connections:

It is one of the many things that social media does. It allows you to form new connections with people.

As I have said, social media is one place where you can share your thoughts and opinions more vividly than ever. Thus, it allows you to find people with similar interests and befriend them.

It is actually very easy to do. You can easily check out the interests and likes of people from their social media profiles. It allows you to understand what an individual is like overall.

Once you have understood that, you can follow them and interact with them to result in a beautiful friendship.

Some might prove to be a really trusted confidante while others might really help you out in your business.

Communicating with people not only opens the door to a healthy lifestyle but also opens opportunities. You might be sitting in your country and signing a business deal with a Facebook friend overseas. Be it related to your personal happiness or growing your business through your social media friends, social media has become a portal where anything and everything is possible.

We need to surround ourselves with people to become truly happy in life. No one can actually live a lonely life and be happy with it. That's human nature!

Social media allows you to overcome social barriers and find new friends as well as create beautiful relationships.

All you need to do is to look for people you find interesting and connect with them. Social media helps you do that.

3

UTILIZING SOCIAL MEDIA: HOW YOU CAN MAKE YOUR VOICE HEARD

"How can you squander even one more day not taking advantage of the greatest shifts of our generation? How dare you settle for less when the world has made it so easy for you to be remarkable?"

- Seth Godin, sethgodin.com

One cannot deny the fact that human beings are the most intelligent creatures on earth. They move ahead in life by interacting with each other and forming connections. So, it is easily understandable that every individual has their own opinion and perspective about life.

We all are born with a certain level of intellect. As a result, each one of us has the power to analyze different situations and take the right decision for ourselves.

Our ability to harbor an opinion is not limited to our personal lives. It rather spans across all the things that we experience in our surroundings. And this quality to have an opinion is something that makes us human beings.

However, the world has changed a lot throughout the years. And until social media, it was becoming more and more difficult to express your opinion about something. Though the constitutions of most countries in this modern world talk about freedom of speech, it is not always easy to express your opinion.

Intolerance is spreading like wildfire across society. In many cases, sharing your opinion has become very difficult. Why? Since many people have become highly intolerant, you can end up being highly criticized if your opinion does not match the general notion of society. You can even become subject to public harassment. But above everything else, you need a platform where you can tell your story to a wide audience.

While it might have seemed impossible even a few years back to have a platform that will help you make your voice and opinions heard, it does not seem impossible nowadays.

Why do I say that? The reason is very simple and we do have social media to thank for providing us with a platform to express our voices. Social media is undoubtedly one of the most important inventions of the modern world.

If you consider the incidents that appear regularly on social media, then the miraculous accomplishments that it helps people achieve will restore your faith in humanity.

Humans of Bombay is a very popular page that has been

putting up life stories of different individuals. One such story was about a 25-year-old man who was suffering from cancer and needed a bone marrow transplant.

Well, his father's bone marrow matched his, however, they were falling short of 25 lakhs (around $35,000) to complete the transplant.

But soon after the young man's story was shared on Humans of Bombay's Facebook page, the netizens helped to raise Rs 25 lakhs in just a day. Surprising, right?

That's the power of social media! It creates impact and changes lives for better or worse. The path you will select, rests upon you.

Yes, if you are commenting on something that you have faced and if it is really sensitive, then social media can make your story go viral. Once it goes viral, it will then be shared across social media platforms until it reaches the right people. In other words, social media gives the power to you. It enables you to express your opinions more openly than ever. And it also gives you the power to take your story to the people and authorities alike with just a simple post.

Now, let us dig in deep to help you understand all the concepts as clearly as possible.

Social media: A tool for the people, by the people, of the people

Back in the day, it was not easy to make your voice heard. If you needed to show your concern or express your opinion on a certain matter, you would have to go to great lengths to do so.

If you think deeply, there were actually very few ways to do it. To mention one, you could send a letter to the editor of a popular newspaper expressing your views. But there was no guarantee that it would be featured in the newspaper since it was completely dependent on whether it would be picked by the editor of the newspaper.

Second, you could write a letter to the appropriate authorities to take action on the matter. However, there was no assurance that they would respond to your letter and take action. Plus, these were long-term processes. So, you had no way to know if or when you would get a fitting response.

But those days are long gone. You no longer need to go through such hassles to make your voice heard. All you have to do is make a post with all the relevant details and you will get a response much sooner than you would expect.

No matter how sensitive the issue is, you will be able to make your voice heard irrespective of all the hurdles. Social media gives you that opportunity. It has become a pillar of democracy that gives a new definition to the concept of freedom of speech.

Plus, social media provides you with the ability of tagging. If you want to express your views about a certain someone or you want to ask the right questions to the right authorities, you can easily do so by tagging the concerned body in your post.

As a result, you will not have to wait for a long time, neither do you need to worry about getting your opinions heard. Just a single post can do all the hard work for you. That is what the creators of the social media platform originally intended to provide people with.

It is a platform "for the people, by the people and of the people." So, you never need to think that you are powerless, as social media offers you the strength to bring about a change in society.

Famous Ethiopian statesman **Haile Selassie** once said: *"Throughout history, it has been the inaction of those who could have acted; the indifference of those who should have known better; the silence of the voice of justice when it mattered most; that has made it possible for evil to triumph."*

What he said is very bitter to hear, but actually showcases an ugly truth of society. Often we common people are silent as a great injustice continues. In the past, a movement for change might take a long time to succeed, or might even be suppressed.

For example, consider the pivotal movement for women's rights, which started when social media, internet and even computers were non-existent.

Today, social media has made the process easier; you have only to look at the #MeToo campaign to see how. It garnered support from different communities, religions, regions and individuals and helped in putting up a strong fight. It's the magic of social media!

All of us have been dominated by the top of the societal hierarchy for quite some time. Now, it is time to bring about change.

It is now time to let the world know that the common people are not sheep that do not have any voice and can be dominated by the people with power.

Now, we have the power to raise our voices. Now, we have the ability to bring about a change and play an important role in making the world a better place for us as well as future generations. Our time has come. And we have social media to thank for it since it has given us the power to make the change.

A platform to raise your voice:

It's time we realize how blessed we are! We have all the opportunities, all the mediums and all the support to make things happen.

We share photos, videos or status updates to last in the memories of our social media family even when we are gone.

So why can't we just use social media to actually mend people's lives?

Be it supporting women's empowerment or voicing against any injustice, let all our posts have some sort of story that will bring meaning to the life of one or many individuals. Even funny cat or dog videos can bring joy.

Social media is a transparent platform. It has billions of participants across the globe. So, you can obviously understand the huge scale of audience that you have available. Social media is no longer limited to its envisaged function of simply connecting people with one another. It rather has fueled a movement to provide the people with the power to express their opinions and their thoughts as clearly as possible.

No matter what peril you face, you now have the opportunity to protest against it and inform others as well as the right authorities by writing a single post. You no longer need to wait for getting approval from other authorities to do so. You no longer need to try to get the attention of newspapers or TV stations, which pursue only a limited number of issues.

Even if you want to suggest or complain about something to the top leader of a country, you will be able to do so by simply writing a post and tagging the social media profile of the president or prime minister. And if you are doing so then you can obviously expect a response. Why am I giving this assurance? Well, when you are making a post like this, it no longer remains private. It is seen by countless numbers of people.

No matter how powerful the authority is, they understand public pressure and are bound to provide an appropriate response to it. So, it will not be wrong to say that social media has given a new dimension to the meaning of democracy.

To simplify it, let's lay down a concept for you.

This incident happened a year ago and it completely changed the way I look at social media. I bought a mobile phone from a nearby showroom. My old phone was broken. So, I decided to get a new one. I had researched quite a bit before deciding on what to buy. After thorough research, I decided to buy Samsung Galaxy S9 Plus. I was really attracted by the features that the phone was offering.

So, one fine day, I went to a nearby Samsung showroom and bought the phone that I was looking forward to buying. They demonstrated everything and the phone seemed okay.

But the trouble started as I came back home. Within a few days, I could see that the smartphone was not working in the way it was supposed to. The display was problematic. The battery was draining out in no time. It didn't take me long to understand that the salespeople in the showroom had handed me a faulty model.

Naturally, I looked for a replacement. It had been just two days since I bought the mobile phone. So I had not violated any warranty regulations. And a phone can be replaced easily.

I went to the store with the bill and all the accessories to ask for a replacement. However, the store manager denied it!

They even did not agree to have a look at my phone. I was told adamantly that I might have done something wrong which created these problems. So I would not get any replacement. They also suggested that I go to the service center to see whether the personnel there could help me out.

I was completely bamboozled. In fact, I did not know what I could do. I had lost a lump sum of money without getting any resolution of my issues.

This naturally made me very depressed and completely hopeless. I told my friend about the incident and asked him for advice.

"Why don't you tweet about it? And make sure you tag the consumer forum to your tweet," my friend said.

At first, I was honestly very suspicious about it. "How will that help when the store officials have refused to replace the phone?" I asked in a low voice.

"Do as I say. You will thank me later," my friend said.

Though skeptical, I went with his advice. I made the tweet about how much I paid, the problems and the harassment I faced. And I tagged the consumer forum to the post. Once I made the tweet, I logged out of Twitter.

After a few hours, when I logged back in, I saw that my post was trending. It had got several retweets and people were actually talking about it.

On the very same day, I also got a reply from the consumer forum saying that they were looking into the matter.

I got really excited as I was sure that something was about to happen.

Within two days, I got a call from the manager of the said Samsung store apologizing for the inconvenience that they had caused. He also asked me to come to their store to receive the replacement.

Well, you might have guessed the rest. My phone was replaced and I am using it to this day without any complaint.

But this incident made me believe in social media. It made me realize how powerful this platform actually is. And what it can actually do for you if you utilize it justly.

"Social media is the ultimate equalizer. It gives a voice and

a platform to anyone willing to engage." — **Amy Jo Martin,** a popular American author, clearly speaks the truth.

Obviously, if you want to raise your voice; if you want your voice to be heard, then social media can help you to do so without any hassle. It has given the power to the people and it rests on how you use it. So, do not be afraid to make your voice heard and make good use of social media.

THE BAD
AND THE UGLY:
DISADVANTAGES OF
SOCIAL MEDIA

4

HOW SOCIAL MEDIA IS RUINING YOUR VALUABLE TIME

"When it comes to social media, there are just times I turn off the world, you know. There are just some times you have to give yourself space to be quiet, which means you've got to set those phones down."

— Michelle Obama

Social media is undoubtedly one of the greatest inventions of the twenty-first century. Social media platforms have not only provided us with a medium to share our thoughts and opinions but have also helped us get connected with others. While social media has a bright positive side, the negative effects of social media have started to concern many people across the globe.

But how is social media affecting your life? What are these adverse effects?

Multiple studies conducted in the last few years have proven that social media acts as a great distraction and it prevents you from realizing your goals. Nowadays, it is not hard to find people who spend much of the time on their mobile devices or computer using social media. It is one of the most common things to see in the world today.

No matter where you are, you will see people remaining engaged in social media without paying attention to the happenings of the real world.

Well, it is true that social media lets you connect with other people and socialize. It also acts as a platform for common people to raise their voice and present their opinions. But there is a downside. When you become too socially active in social media, you stop providing much time to realize your own goals.

Social media binds you like any other addiction and you start to stumble in the road of your life. Once you are totally addicted to social media, it becomes too hard to get out of it.

You always feel the strong urge to check out your social media feeds to see everything that has been happening out there. In the process, you end up losing much of your valuable time.

"Time and tide wait for no one" - this is perhaps one of the most common proverbs that we are all familiar with. The river of time continues to flow without being interrupted by anyone or anything. As a result, you will end up losing your precious time before you can even realize it.

We all have our own dreams and ambitions. We all work hard to make them a reality and become successful in life. However, to make that happen, you will have to take the right step at the right time.

What happens if you end up losing time?

Once the right time has passed, it becomes very hard to get your life back on track. Life does not give you second chances all the time. Hence, if you have lost time then you end up being a loser. So, you will always have to work hard and remain vigilant to utilize the time as well as the opportunities you get.

Social media, on the other hand, can create a great imbalance in all of these. With all the things that it offers, it becomes too hard to ignore it. And once you become fully engaged, it becomes too hard to get out of the bindings of social media.

While it is true that limited use of social media is necessary to stay updated in the world today, the real problem begins when you start to overuse it and become addicted to social media.

Now that I have explained how social media is ruining your time as well as your life, it is time to understand how you can cut your social media consumption and focus on realizing your goals.

The very first thing that you need to cut your social media

usage and utilize your time well is self-determination and self-control. In other words, you need to build up your mental strength to get out of this addiction.

Obviously, you will always feel this incredible urge to check out your phone from time to time and see what is happening. But you will have to stop yourself from doing that if you want to achieve your goals. And of course, it requires sheer strength of mind.

From what we have discussed so far, it is completely clear that our end goal is to limit the usage of social media in order to utilize our time properly. Well, one of the best ways to do that is create self-rule and limit the time that you can spend on social media.

If you are looking for a drastic change in just a day, then I must tell you that most likely it is not possible. Even if you uninstall the social media apps from your smartphone, in most cases your plan will fail.

You will not be able to overcome your urge to check in on your social profiles that quickly. So, the right thing to do is to decrease the time that you spend on social media gradually.

As I said, you can create self-rule and impose it on yourself to decrease your social media usage. But how will you do it? Well, it is very simple. You will have to assign a time limit for using social media in a day and follow it earnestly. You will have to slowly decrease the limit with the passage of time in order to get yourself totally out of social media addiction.

Furthermore, you also need to ask yourself why you are using social media and what you want to achieve from it.

Are you using it to spend time with your friends or people close to you? To meet new people? Or to enhance the growth of your business by utilizing this massive platform?

Once you ask yourself these questions and try to answer them, it will automatically click for you how much time you are losing. Thus, you will be able to take the necessary action to get out of it.

Having said that, I will still say that it requires sheer willpower and strength of character to achieve this feat. And in this chapter, I will help you to achieve that strategically.

"It takes discipline not to let social media steal your time." — **Alexis Ohanian**, an American business mogul, beautifully summarized everything that I have been trying to say up till this point.

Discipline is one of the most important things in life. Without proper discipline, it is impossible to be successful. And that applies to using social media too. If you are not disciplined enough, if you do not have proper control over yourself, then you will never be able to stop social media from ruining your valuable time.

But how will you discipline yourself? How will you protect yourself from being trapped by the endless lure of social media? Well, I will help you to do that in this chapter.

In the past 40 years of my life, I have had many experiences and witnessed several ups and downs in my path. And I persevered through all of it to reach the position where I am today.

Though I have tried to lead a disciplined life all along, I have also not been able to keep myself out of the trap of social media and the internet overall. I had to work hard to bring back the discipline and stop social media platforms from wasting my precious time.

So, whatever I am going to suggest to you, it comes out of my own personal experience and extensive research on the subject. So, all aboard the train and let's stop social media from stealing your precious time.

Set the Golden Rule:

Yes, of course, this is the very first step that you need to take to stop social media from wasting your precious time.

But what is the golden rule? What do I mean by saying this?

Well, the answer is very simple. I have already informed you about the self-rule that you need to impose to prevent you from losing time using social media. The concept of the golden rule is similar.

If you spend too much time on social media and you can understand the detrimental effects on your life, setting up self-rule can help you a lot.

The concept is very easy. And you should not have any trouble practicing it. Imposing self-rule has always been considered one of the ways to keep yourself from unnecessary attractions. And it can help you with this too.

So, what do you need to do?

Well, if you currently spend several hours a day on social media and it is affecting your career as well as your life, then just create self-rule. Stand in front of a mirror and promise to yourself that you will not use social media more than a stipulated time (which you set for yourself).

You can personalize the rule. For example, you can promise yourself you will not be engaged in social media once you reach home after work. And you will invest the time in your family and in realizing your goals.

Once you set the rule, you will have to follow it with utmost sincerity. If you fail somewhere, ask yourself why you failed and how you can get it right the next time.

One way to keep yourself motivated is to take a jar and put a label on it. Every time you fail, just put a good amount of money in it. Once you start following this rule, you will be able to keep yourself motivated and prevent yourself from indulging in social media all the time. In fact, you can use it for a good cause. Maybe donate it and help people who are actually in need. In short, use the money for a social cause only.

Let me tell you a personal story to help you realize the concept.

This incident happened a year ago and really made me question the usefulness of social media overall.

We are a family of five. One day, I returned from the office and I did not get the usual greetings from my kids. They were busy using social media on their mobiles.

I went up to them and heard: "Hi, Dad."

Taken aback, I said, "Hi."

I went up to my wife. She was sitting on the couch with her mobile in her hand.

"The girls are in some mood today, huh?" I told my wife.

"Uh-huh," she replied, being too busy to even respond correctly.

I did not say anything and went to freshen up. After freshening up, I sat on my bed and opened my mobile.

I was browsing through Facebook as I used to do every day. Suddenly, I came across a meme. It was ironic as well as funny at the same time.

The picture depicted a deep pit into which people are falling. On one side of the pit, it was labeled "ME." The pit was labeled "Social Media." And the other side of the pit said "My Life Goals and Expectations."

I found it very funny and laughed a little. I shared the meme on my Instagram profile. Instantly, I saw myself in the mirror with my phone in my hand. It suddenly came to me.

I asked myself: "What am I doing? I am not different from the people depicted in the picture."

I realized how I was wasting my precious time using social media without spending time with my family or achieving my goals.

It came as a surprise and I was shocked to see what I had become.

I rushed to my wife and told her about what I just realized. After listening to my words, she was equally shocked and perplexed. We apologized to each other and talked to the kids about it to help them understand how social media was stealing our time.

We set up our golden rule and decided to not spend more than an hour on social media so that we could spend as much time as we could with each other and our work.

We also picked up a jar and labeled it "Penalty Jar." We decided that if any one of us was found using social media for more than an hour then we would put ₹100 (over $1) as a fine in the jar.

The plan worked and within a few months, we were back to our normal selves being a happy family.

"I was too busy. But with what? I constantly obsessed over what other people—many of them complete strangers—were posting on Facebook, Instagram, Snapchat, or my fraternity group chat. My time was being eroded by a hundred little distractions every day. I was literally clicking my life away." — **A.N. Turner,** author of the bestselling book *Trapped in the Web,* wrote this in his book. And he absolutely told the truth in his book.

It clearly explains how deep and harmful social media addiction is. We all use it as a way to get some recreation after a long day of work.

However, unknowingly, it becomes a major addiction

which slowly steals our precious time and turns us into nothing but losers.

If you really want to stop that, then you will have to fight for it. You will have to fight against the undeniable desire to open your social media application and check on what others are posting.

Truth be told, this is not an easy feat to achieve. As I said before, it requires sheer power of will and moral strength to fight off the lure and stop social media from ruining your valuable time.

But if you try hard and follow the steps above, you will be able to fend off the social media addiction and focus on your goals.

"It's so funny how social media was just this fun thing, and now it's this monster that consumes so many millennial lives." — **Cazzie David,** an American actor, said this and it is absolutely true.

Fight the monster, set up your golden rule and be disciplined to achieve success in life.

5

SOCIAL MEDIA: A HURDLE IN THE PATH OF ACHIEVING A SUCCESSFUL LIFE??

"Social media policies will never be able to cure stupid."

— Nichole Kelly

We live in a world where social media has gained unparalleled importance. Today, most people are connected to all the social media platforms. Social media was developed as a medium for us to connect with others. It was supposed to be a platform that would help us make new friends, connect with our close ones and meet new people. However, it did not quite pan out as expected.

Social media nowadays has become a place where people criticize one another and express their opinions of others without even knowing them.

But the repercussions of social media are not constrained

to criticizing others. They are far graver than what you can even fathom.

Have you ever stopped to think whether social media is ruining your life?

Have you ever thought that social media can play a big part in preventing you from achieving your goals?

Well, we generally don't pay much attention to all this and that is where most of us go wrong.

Let's take a look back at our life before all the digital platforms that ever existed. Being a person who himself belongs to generation X, I can say that life was much more carefree. We didn't have to worry about what to post and what not!

In fact, we believed in listening, feeling, communicating and establishing our presence in someone's life. And that too not virtually.

The habit of not responding to a person and staying engaged in your device is the first step where you have gone wrong.

Undoubtedly, social media has been proven as one of the biggest hurdles in the path of achieving success in life because people are not communicating or interacting.

But why? Why am I saying that social media acts as a hurdle?

Well, there are several reasons behind the statement I am making. It truly is a big hurdle in your life. Feeling a little confused? Let me explain everything to you.

As I have mentioned in a previous chapter, social media is highly addictive. And it is no less harmful than any other addiction. Since most people these days are suffering from social media addiction, they rush towards their mobile phones or other devices as soon as they wake up from their night's sleep to check their social media feeds and see what others are posting.

If asked, most people will say they feel an unbearable need to check their social media feeds as soon as they wake up. That's how grave social media addiction really is.

In reality, social media is making most of us more interested in others' lives than our own. We are constantly judging others by their posts and in return, we are constantly being judged too. This is a vicious cycle that never ends and we get trapped in it.

We concentrate so much on others' lives that we forget our own goals and the milestones that we always wanted to achieve. Furthermore, social media is also making us completely dependent on the opinion of others.

Yes, it is completely true. Whenever we post photos or status, we always crave others' approval. You work hard to mold yourself into a being who can stand high in the opinion of others and become popular on social media.

That's the sad reality of our society today and there is nothing that can be done unless people understand how they are failing in their real life in order to become successful in the digital one.

Now, let me come back to the point where I started. So, how does social media pose a threat to your journey to achieve success in life? It is not complicated at all to figure out the answer from everything that I have said so far. The answer is quite simple indeed.

The very first thing that addiction to social media does to you is to rob you of your valuable time. Yes, you lose a lot of time in your day in surfing through your social media feeds and making interesting posts.

Time is undoubtedly the most essential as well as the truest thing in the universe. It goes by at an incredible speed and once it has passed there is no way to turn back the wheel of time. So, it is essential to utilize your time carefully and work hard if you really want to achieve success in life.

But how will you utilize your time and realize when an opportunity has come your way when you are too busy with your social media affairs? Well, it may look very sad but it is the real truth. People nowadays are so addicted to the numerous social media platforms that they completely forget their real-life goals and concentrate more on gaining popularity on social media.

In other words, you get so addicted to getting likes and new followers in your social media accounts that you completely forget that you have a real life and you have your own ambitions that you need to fulfill.

As this addiction continues, you keep losing your own time until you realize one day that you have lost all your opportunities and have turned yourself into nothing but a failure. An outcome like this can be obviously very cruel. But that is what social media does. It robs you of the most important thing in your life: time. Above all, it breaks your self-confidence since you are controlled by what others think of you on social media.

Self-confidence is undoubtedly one of the most important qualities that every person needs to become successful in life. If you are not confident about yourself then no one else is going to put their confidence in you and that is how the cycle of life works.

However, social media is destroying the self-worth of its users. You become a puppet trying to impress others by molding yourself to their likings without thinking of your own individuality. In the process, you keep losing one of the biggest assets you have: your self-confidence. Let me explain this to you with an appropriate example.

Suppose you are posting a photo of yourself on one of your social media accounts. You click the photo in an appropriate pose and edit it as required to post it. After posting the photo, the first comment you get is from one of your followers criticizing the way you look. Instantly, you get upset and take actions to improve the way you look in your pictures.

Well, this is something very common among social media

users. We constantly depend on the opinion of others. We fail to form our own opinions and stick by them. That is the harsh reality of the modern age.

As a result, you get greatly invested in pleasing others and improving their opinions about you. Yes, you constantly crave their approval. On the other hand, you overlook your own goals and fail to walk on the path of life to achieve success confidently.

Lives of millennials are now more about growing socially. However, it has even affected generation X. My best friend now prefers watching Netflix on a Sunday night over a road trip with friends. Success comes with self-determination, as well as with the support and encouragement of the people around us. But now we are channeling that determination into getting more views on Snapchat, curating an Instagrammable post and so on.

Don't get me wrong, if you can cash out the posts on your social media platforms, then you have successfully started your journey towards making money through digital marketing. But in most cases, it's just for getting social approval.

To be specific, I have seen my sister getting happy over getting a "you are looking beautiful in this dress" comment on her Instagram post. This cultivated the urge to make more social media posts in order to get compliments. Whereas real-life compliments don't seem to matter.

Success comes with having both real-life and online connections side by side.

But now the question is how will you get past this hurdle in your path to achieve success? How will you become successful in life without being tempted by the lures of social media? Well, the answer is pretty simple.

Getting used to a certain social media image is common. But to have a bigger focus and goals, you need to do two things.

So, what are these two things?

The very first thing is to decide which posts deserve a share. Ask yourself whether the post is too personal. Set a privacy bar and try not to cross that. Making every little problem or personal moment public is certainly the worst thing you can do.

Second, you need to get out of being controlled by others' opinions and build up your own self-confidence.

But how will you achieve it? Well, I am here to help you out. In this chapter, I will show you how to overthrow the hurdle of social media and help you to achieve success.

Go by the rules: Utilize your time perfectly:

"You've got to know what you want. This is central to acting on your intentions. When you know what you want, you realize that all there is left then is time management. You'll manage your time to achieve your goals because you clearly know what you're trying to achieve in your life." — **Patch Adams**, a popular

American author, said this in an interview, and it beautifully outlines the importance of time management.

Focus on some flashbacks. Try to remember how many special moments were just crushed because of intrusive social media. Why do we always feel the need for documenting life live on social media?

Let's face it, there is just no need to give out each and every detail to your followers.

Life before social media had that mystery! There was absolutely no competition over dining at the most Instagram-worthy restaurant or flaunting your look for the day. It was all a personal choice. For example, the famous poet William Wordsworth (1770-1850) found joy in direct experiences.

There is no need to quit social media platforms forever. But measures can be taken.

Set the rules first by charting out a social media menu. Yes! A menu that will state as well as monitor your social media activities. I personally have tried it and honestly, even the user's ego stays satisfied.

While preparing this menu, you have the liberty to chart it out however you like. It definitely gives you free choice to make alterations as needed and you can't blame other individuals for formulating it for you.

Say, for instance, you want to spend more time on YouTube and Instagram and cut short on other apps. However, the deal is that you get a specific time slot for these apps and the remaining time will be spent away from these social media platforms.

Sound simple yet challenging?

Well, the mission of this menu is to make you win at the end of the day. You have the opportunity to spend time on social media as well as other things.

This process of social media detoxification has to be done in a progressive way. That means you will have to decrease social media usage slowly but steadily by taking small and simple steps.

But why do you need to take small steps? Why can't you reduce social media usage drastically?

Well, it sounds fantastic but it is not practical at all. Like every other addiction, you cannot get rid of social media addiction drastically in a day. It takes proper discipline and control over your own self to actually get out of the addiction.

Let me tell you one of my own experiences to clearly illustrate the concept.

Throughout my life, I have always considered the fact that time is equal to success. If you lose time, then you will never be able to achieve success in your life.

Despite being disciplined throughout my life, I also could not overcome the allure of social media. I became addicted to it. Though I did not realize it at first but when the realization came, it really made me frustrated.

One day I was sitting in my office surfing Facebook, suddenly one of my employees entered my office.

"Sir, server one is not responding," he said while gasping to catch a breath.

The matter was serious as several of our customers' websites ran in this server.

"Fix it immediately," I said without moving my eyes from my mobile. I failed to realize how important the matter was since I was completely concentrating on my mobile.

The employee went away. I was so deeply immersed in my mobile that I completely forgot about the matter.

I went back home without paying any heed to it. The problem that one of my staffers told me about had completely washed out of my brain.

The very next day when I entered my office, I realized how grave my mistake was.

Our systems were flooding with messages from our angry customers. I immediately rushed to my maintenance team to see how the repair of the server was coming.

The situation was grave. The work was progressing slowly. I realized the mistake I had made. If I had paid attention when I was being briefed about the problem, I could have asked the maintenance team to work overnight to fix it. I could have stayed along with them and shared my insights to help them speed up the process.

I had lost 14-15 hours which made the situation much

more serious. If I could have been a little bit more attentive, I would not have made this mistake.

I could not help but feel terrible. From that moment, I swore to utilize my time perfectly without wasting it on social media. I promised myself not to use social media more than an hour a day.

I always tried to remain true to the promise I made to myself, though I had to repeat it at times, and eventually I was able to get rid of my social media addiction. As a result, once again I was utilizing my time properly and I was able to get back on the right track towards realizing my goals.

"I think time management as a label encourages people to view each 24-hour period as a slot in which they should pack as much as possible." — **Tim Ferriss**, a celebrated author of our times, said this. It beautifully depicts how important it is to utilize your time well.

Be confident and utilize your time perfectly without letting your social media addiction take over. Live a disciplined life and control the usage of social media completely. Do not let it ruin your self-confidence.

6

TECHNOLOGY EQUALS MORE PRODUCTIVITY! IS IT A BUBBLE OF A LIE?

"Privacy is dead, and social media holds the smoking gun."

— **Pete Cashmore,** Mashable CEO

The history of human civilization is a history of technological advancements. From learning to harness fire and making wheels to building the highly advanced digital technology that we now use in our everyday lives, the human race has made marvelous achievements in the field of technology.

We have made communication very easy with our mobile phones. We have explored the depths of space by building spaceships. In other words, we can say technology has brought a new dimension to our lives.

Often, we hear that technology equals more productivity.

This is the common notion among us. But is it really true? Does technology really help us to be more productive? Well, it is true that we benefit from a lot of technological advancements. And there is no denying that it has increased our work efficiency and productivity to a great extent.

But here a question arises! Does every technological advance help us to be more productive? To be precise, does social media help us to be more productive? The answer to this question is sadly no. It does not help us to be more productive.

While there are many who will disagree with me and it will spark hot debates, it is the truth. Social media does not help us to be more productive rather it serves as a distraction and make us waste our valuable time.

Social media is considered by many to be one of the greatest inventions of modern times. It was originally designed with the intention of helping people connect with each other. However, over the course of time and modifications to the social media platform, it has become a distraction for humankind. And there is no denying it.

You can't help but be surrounded by multiple distractions. It's tempting, it's damaging and it will keep you detached from experiencing real life.

But I have always realized that it's the thought of confronting real life without social media that holds us back. Well, let me tell you, real life may be dull, it may not be the most happening one, but it will certainly not be controlled by any social media app.

My suggestion: control your social media addiction before it starts overpowering you.

"It's so funny how social media was just this fun thing, and now it's this monster that consumes so many millennial lives." — **Cazzie David**, an American actor and entertainer, said this in an interview. Sadly, it is completely true.

What's scarier than being dead? Being judged!

Social media asks you to judge others or vice versa. But that was all fun before, right? Or just when it was only among friends?

Well sadly, it's not the case anymore. Having the thought of waking up to bad comments or fewer likes compared to other posts definitely gives millennials a sleepless night.

It has become a monster that has implemented a different idea of self-love. And it's just counted through likes, comments and shares.

"The bad news is time flies. The good news is you're the pilot." — **Michael Altshuler**, a world-famous motivational speaker, said it well.

However, most of us fail to truly understand his meaning. We spend countless hours surfing through our social media newsfeed without actually realizing everything that we can achieve if we really utilize the time that we are wasting.

Back in the day, all we wanted to do was go out and play. We were active, we weren't too lethargic to explore more and most importantly, we were fit.

But soon our attention got divided with the introduction of video games. Well, it is true that video games are really addictive, however, we hadn't given up on outdoor games. Finally came the era when online games prevailed.

In this present era, a huge percentage of children are involved in social media gaming, so much that they have failed to develop energy for playing any sort of outdoor game.

Similarly, social media even affects the health of adults. As per the *Journal of the American Medical Association*, our average daily sitting time has witnessed a massive increase from 5.5 to 6.4 hours in adults and as much as 7.0 to 8.2 among children. Shocking, right?

This makes us more prone to heart disease, cancer and so many other health issues.

Do you seriously want to be a part of such an unhealthy and inactive lifestyle? And put the lives of our kids in danger too?

Think! Rethink!

We are spending the peak time of our lives going through our social feeds. Have you ever realized what you could achieve if you do not waste your time so carelessly? Sadly, most of us do not. We do not comprehend how serious the repercussions of social media addiction are.

We go on wasting our time on this platform until one day when an incident makes us realize how much damage social media has done. This is the reality of social media. Most interestingly, it has been found in studies that the youth of today are not only the ones that are being affected by social media. It affects people belonging to all age groups. So, you can obviously understand how serious the matter is.

Anthony Carmon, a respected Trinidadian statesman, once said, *"Social media websites are no longer performing an envisaged function of creating a positive communication link among friends, family and professionals. It is a veritable battleground, where insults fly from the human quiver, damaging lives, destroying self-esteem and a person's sense of self-worth."*

The quote above beautifully explains the point that I have been trying to prove all along. Social media not only affects our productivity but it also affects our self-esteem greatly. As I said before, we constantly seek approval from others for everything. In other words, we are becoming more and more dependent on the opinion of other people.

We forget what we need to do and the targets that we need to achieve. We would rather work hard to build a great image in social media and make ourselves popular among others.

But that should not be the case. If you really want to achieve your goals, you need to increase your productivity and work efficiency without being distracted by something like social media. In fact, use social media as a tool to grow your business and obtain new customers.

Make the most out of the platform that can gain business for you. This is the oath that every one of us should take. And every one of us needs to work hard to make sure that we can achieve our goals without wasting time on social media.

However, it is no easy feat to achieve. You need to have extreme self-control and strength of character to cut back on your social media usage. Yes, it takes a lot of self-control to overlook your social media cravings and keep your focus intact on your work. Thus, it becomes very hard for most people to actually achieve this feat.

But how will you do it? We will discuss some good tactics for controlling social media use in this chapter.

Set the rules straight! Let go of the ego

You might be wondering how ego is related to our social media addiction. Do you feel the need to receive more likes or comments than everyone else? Does it worry you when your Instagram post doesn't get the expected reach and your likes get stuck?

If yes, here lies the problem. Our ego wants us to be above all, even when we know that it might be realistic. To be on top compared to others in social media is the motivation of our ego. To be sad when the follower count is not increasing or when we are getting less likes doesn't appease our ego.

So first, we have to let it go.

"Astonishingly, the average person will spend nearly two hours (approximately 116 minutes) on social media every day, which translates to a total of 5 years and 4 months spent over a lifetime. Even more, time spent on social media is only expected to increase as platforms develop." - A clear depiction is given by *Social Media Today*. And it accurately gives us a picture of the havoc social media addiction is creating.

So, you can obviously understand how much you can achieve if you do not lose 5 years of your time in social media. Being productive does not mean only finishing the work that has been assigned to you. It means achieving your own personal goals and facilitating your personal development. And it can only be done when you can focus on your targets completely without losing time.

Now, the question is how to control your social media usage? Well, one of the very first things that you can do is to keep yourself engaged in work without being distracted by social media.

From personal life to professional work, you must first separate your priorities. Focus on accomplishing all your professional tasks back at your workspace. But whenever you are home, dedicate yourself to your family and spend maximum time with them. If you continuously stay engaged in something, then the urge to constantly check your phone soon will be gone.

Though it sounds like a very easy thing to do, that is never the case. It takes a lot of self-control and discipline to keep yourself away from the fanciful world of social media. And this is not something that I am quoting from a textbook. I am saying it out of the experience that I have gathered in the 40 years of my life. So, let me tell you about that experience to help you understand the concept in a much better way.

The incident that I am going to narrate happened a few years back. I had always been very fond of social media up till then. I used to spend a long time on my social media accounts posting about my daily exploits and checking on my friends.

However, I never realized the fact that I was losing a lot of time. Like almost everyone else, I never thought about it really.

My life was going quite well. I was unaware of the troubles that were waiting for me. Excessive social media usage actually warped my sense of punctuality and productivity greatly.

I used to start my day by surfing my Facebook and Instagram accounts. The pompous world of social media used to attract me like a magnet attracts a piece of iron.

Throughout my life, I have always tried to live with the utmost discipline. But my social media addiction was creating problems for me. I would be late for my office and my commitments. I stopped paying close attention to the problems of my family and company. Furthermore, I started living in my own fictional world thanks to my social media addiction. I had to have the best posts and garner more likes and comments. That seemed to become my main aim. As a result, I would often forget many important things since I was concentrating on social media more than anything else.

It continued for a long time until one day I understood my mistake.

I was sitting on my couch and surfing through my Facebook profile on a Sunday morning.

Suddenly, my elder daughter came and said: "Papa, I have a math test in two days. And there is one chapter that I am not getting the solutions easily. Will you help me with that?"

"Of course, sweetie. It is no big deal. I will show you how to do those sums once I am free. They are very easy.

Do not worry," I replied without turning my gaze from my mobile phone.

Naturally, I was so engrossed in social media that I did not pay much heed to it. So, I completely forgot about her math test.

Two days later, I had just returned home from my office and planted myself on my couch. Suddenly, I noticed that my elder daughter's room was closed from inside. It was really surprising as she never keeps her door closed especially during the time when I come back from my office. She is usually the one who runs into my arms and greets me when I return. It was really odd to me.

I called my wife and asked why our daughter was keeping her door closed. And what she told me struck me very hard. She told me that my daughter performed poorly on her math test since I was too busy with my phone to help her out. That was why she was upset and had kept her door closed since she had returned from school.

I understood my mistake and it completely filled me with grief. I understood how unproductive I had become and how much harm it was causing.

So, I instantly made up my mind and cut my social media usage to one-fifth of what it used to be. And I followed this rule with utmost sincerity.

It brought a great change to my life. I instantly became more efficient, attentive and productive. Thus, it became easy for me to pay attention to what others say and remain focused on my goals.

Since then I have never let down my daughter or anyone else again. I increased my productivity greatly and kept on achieving new milestones in my life.

Be serious about your work:

Of course, this is one of the foremost things that we need to achieve to become successful in our lives. We need to be completely serious about the work that we do. And that is the way to increase our productivity greatly.

Most of us fail to understand the importance of the work that we do. It especially happens because social media shapes our perception greatly. We remain so engaged in social media that we completely ignore the work that we need to do, which in return turns us into utter failures.

However, it is not at all easy to remain serious about your work and overlook the strong forces of attraction and intruding notifications from your social media platform.

So, how will you do it? Well, the answer is very simple. You need to completely realize the priority of your time and your work. Most importantly, you have to be completely focused on your work such that social media cannot distract you in any way.

A year back my company got lucky to win a big project. Obviously, it was a do-or-die situation for all my employees and even myself. Ultimatums were given and we had to accomplish the assignment in just a week. And the pressure was beyond expectation.

Amid one of those busy days, I had to leave for a client meeting. It was easier said than done. Well, I ordered my employees to fully focus on this assignment.

However, after just a few minutes, I received a notification on Instagram that my company's manager liked my recent post.

You can say that it's a personal matter and your manager can surf through Instagram whenever needed. Here is where we go wrong. Instagram was designed with the purpose of being a fun app used at leisure times. If managers surf social media platforms during the most crucial times, then what will subordinates learn from them?

I have no problem if my employees stay active in social media while in the office. But only during free time. When the company needs them to stay focused and meet deadlines, they must stay dedicated to accomplishing the given task. You need to be completely disciplined and you must have the strength of character to keep yourself focused on your work.

Killing time by doing nothing is one of the disadvantages of social media. Social media was meant to be used at times when you are bored with doing nothing. It never made it to the market with the intention of killing productivity.

Impose self-rule on yourself as I have discussed above and I guarantee you that you will be able to be more productive and efficient.

7

A LONE WORLD:
IS SOCIAL MEDIA CREATING
DEPRESSION AND ANXIETY?

"Social media, unfortunately, just makes it a lot easier to be jealous. It sets up false expectations of reality, so it's really easy to look at someone else's life online and assume that they have everything going great for them and that their life is perfect."

— **Franchesca Ramsey**

Social media is having a great impact on our society. It has become one of the most common things that we use in our everyday lives. Every time we upload a photo or post a status, we create a digital footprint for ourselves which others can track to get acquainted with us in a better way.

Social media was designed with the goal of connecting like-minded people. However, present circumstances make us question whether that goal is being achieved.

Is social media really performing the way it was meant to? Is it really connecting people? Well, the answer seems to be negative for many. Rather than connecting people, social media is giving rise to social anxiety, jealousy and depression.

This might come as a big shocker. But it is the real truth. Social media has become a prominent reason behind the rising number of mental ailments. Honestly, our selfish desire to achieve popularity in the social media platform has a lot to do with our present-day condition.

Nowadays, most people use the social media platform as a means to promote themselves. Whether you are making a post or sharing one, you always make sure that you establish yourself as the most stylish and the coolest personality on social media. You earnestly keep track of the likes, comments and shares that your posts get. If your post performs well then it certainly provides you with a great extent of joy.

Getting attention and praise in social media has become quite addictive for most people nowadays. You work hard and give a lot of thought to your posts to gain more likes and praise from others. But what happens if one of your posts does not do well? What happens if someone else outsmarts you in this race?

Well, that is where the trouble starts. Whenever one of your posts fails to garner much attention or someone else steals your limelight in social media, it causes you to panic and ultimately pushes you toward depression.

You search anxiously for a way to turn all the attention back to you. Thus, you completely lose your focus from your real life. You develop a form of social anxiety and you start to think of yourself as a social outcast who does not fit in well with others. In fact, you start to live the digital life and try hard to remain popular in every way possible in social media.

On the other hand, it constantly distances you from the reality of life. Though you become a popular name in social media, in real life you end up with anxiety and uneasiness in communicating or interacting with others.

"We live in a culture where everyone's opinion, view, and assessment of situations and people spills across social media, a lot of it anonymously, much of it shaped by mindless meanness and ignorance." — *The famous American journalist* **Mike Barnicle** said this, and no one can deny but to accept that he speaks the truth.

In our earnest efforts to become popular social media personalities, we end up being controlled by the opinions of other people. We end up doing what others want to simply gain likes, comments and followers. But this tendency becomes the reason for the social anxiety that most people have. You get so involved in living the digital life that you end up forgetting how to live your real life. As a result, you end up being a victim of anxiety.

I have also stated previously that social media causes depression. Many people will surely argue over the nature of my statement. However, if you think closely then you will be able to find the reasoning on which I based my statement. You will be able to understand what I am really trying to convey.

Depression is a serious ailment. And to find a cure for this disease is actually very tough. Most people confuse depression with sadness, but it is a much more pressing concern.

As I said, most people today are living a lie. We see people posting different photographs of themselves on Facebook and Instagram at different hours of the day to get likes and followers. Be it photos they have posted just after waking up in the morning or something else, the way they look on these photos always makes us wonder.

"How can someone look so gorgeous just after waking up?" - This is the very first question that comes to your mind after seeing such posts. Well, the answer is very simple. A lot of hard work and makeup goes into creating these photos or posts. Thus, the "good morning" posts where you see others rising from bed with just the perfect look are essentially a lie.

This attention-seeking tendency and over-attachment to the world of social media often becomes the reason behind depression. As I said, you become so involved in living the digital life that you forget the right way to live the real one.

As a result, you end up distancing yourself from the people who care about you in reality. You become lonely and it slowly gives rise to depression. Despite having a stalwart social media following, you turn into a lonely, broken person who masquerades as a completely different person on social media.

The consequences of depression and loneliness are severe. It can even kill you. No matter how you portray yourself in your social media profiles, in reality, you end up being a loser.

But what can you do? How can you get yourself out of the cobweb of social media addiction?

Well, here are some solutions.

Communicate with people in real life:

The heading says it all! It is the best way to get rid of your social anxiety and awkwardness in front of others.

No matter how popular you are on social media, the duality in which you live often gives rise to social anxiety. Though you become popular in the digital world of social media, you forget how to communicate with other people in real life. As a result, you always suffer from anxiety in front of others.

However, the best way to get rid of this anxiety and to put your life back on the right track is to increase your interactions with other people rather than spending time on social media.

Human beings are social animals. We are meant to communicate or interact with others. We are meant to surround ourselves with the people who care about us. And social media addiction becomes a hurdle in this road.

So, the very first thing that you need to do to get rid of your anxiety is to increase real-life interactions with people by reducing your social media usage.

When you start interacting with others, you will instantly notice the difference it makes. Once you start spending time with real people rather than sticking to the screen of your computer or mobile phone, you will be able to get rid of your anxiety slowly. You will become more comfortable in meeting and interacting with other people, which will relieve all your awkwardness as well as palpitations. You will become a much better person than you are at present.

Let me tell you a story to help you understand the concept in a much better way. What I am going to tell you next is based on a true experience that I had a few years back.

My sister has always been one of the most lovely and charming persons that I have ever come across. She was born with an incredible charm. She was very confident and she had the ability to instantly befriend others with her incredible charm. I was always told that I was the shy introvert among us.

But that changed pretty quickly. My sister has been a technology enthusiast from the very beginning. So, when the social media platform started to become a serious thing, she was one of the first to become a part of it.

Within a very short time, she became very popular on social media with several followers and admirers. It did not take her long to become the queen of social media.

But it had a much deeper impact on her than I could ever have imagined. The person who was very charming and loved to interact with others slowly started to isolate herself during social gatherings and parties. She would hardly talk with us anymore. She became so busy with her smartphone and social media that our interactions were reduced to the absolute minimum.

This sudden change concerned me greatly and I did not

know what to do. To be honest, she was slowly moving away from us and I could hardly recognize who she was anymore. My own sister had become a complete stranger to me.

So, I decided to act! I decided to talk to her as soon as possible before it became too late.

I knew she would not be interested in talking to me, especially about this topic. She would lock herself in her room or pretend to be too busy to have a heartfelt conversation with her elder brother.

So I came up with a plan. I took her shopping one day and from there we decided to have lunch at her favorite restaurant.

We sat face to face at a small table for two. There were few people around us there. It was the perfect time to address the elephant in the room.

"What has happened to you, sis? Why did you change so much?" I asked my sister.

She moved her eyes from her phone and made eye contact with me. But she did not say a word. I felt like ages had passed since I interacted with my sister.

"You have always been the star of our house. There was a time, you used to love so much to interact with others. Surprisingly, you have always been the nucleus of our family. With your charm and personality, you would always cheer us up whenever we felt down," I continued.

"What happened to you? I can hardly recognize you anymore. You were always so talkative and full of life. But have you looked at yourself lately? These days, you hardly talk to me anymore. You used to tell me everything before. Now, I hardly get the chance to even talk with my little sister since you are always so busy with your phone," I said.

My sister did not say a word. But I could see that her eyes had become teary. "Ugh. I no longer recognize myself either. Nowadays, I feel anxious as well as awkward to talk with others. I do not know what to say to people anymore," she said in a choked-up voice.

"No, you have not forgotten anything. It is your extreme addiction to social media that is causing all these troubles. If you are always so concerned about empowering your digital life, how will you make time for your real life? The solitary confinement that you forced yourself into is creating all the problems for you. And social media is to blame for this," I said in a concerned voice.

"So, what do I do? How do I get rid of this?" she asked with great concern in her voice.

"Stop using social media so much. Start spending more time with us like you always have. You will notice the difference shortly," I replied, giving an affectionate flick to her forehead.

She did what I asked. And her transformation was incredible. Within a few days, she again became her own self. We had regained the star of the family and I gave a sigh of relief to have my sister back to normal again.

"I just constantly tell myself that I should be the only one to define my worth and what I'm capable of and how I perceive myself. And that I should never source that worth from other people, especially strangers on social media. They don't know

who I am, the length of my journey, who I am as a person." — **Catriona Gray**, a well known Filipino model, said this in an interview, and it is true though it sounds very bitter.

Do not let social media control your life. Surround yourself with others, interact with people in real life and you will be able to get rid of social anxiety and awkwardness.

Surround yourself with people who cherish you:

As I said before, depression is one of the pressing concerns of modern society and social media is fueling it greatly.

Most people live a lie in order to impress others on social media thereby detaching themselves from the people that care in real life. This makes them lonely and severely depressed. As they lose people from their lives and their mental health deteriorates, it soon becomes a major problem which one could hardly anticipate.

If you are suffering from the same problem then I have only one suggestion for you. Stop trying to impress others and start to live your life on your own terms. Surround yourself with people who actually cherish you without trying to be overly popular with a group of strangers.

Depression has the tendency to create a hole in your heart. This hole can only be filled with the people who actually care about and love you. Stop accepting the false standards that social media has created and start spending more time with the people who truly love you. You will be able to feel the difference.

Social media is a tool meant to be connecting people. Do not let it detach you from your loved ones. Live your life to the fullest and do not let social media control you. That is the right way to get rid of loneliness and depression that social media brings.

Is it right to point fingers? Social media not a cause of depression and anxiety?

Previously, I have explained that depression and anxiety are somewhat caused by social media. Not to contradict me, but it differs from person to person. Now if you notice, I have constantly highlighted the point that it's us human beings who get triggered positively or negatively by social media. And then if anything goes wrong, we blame it on social media.

In short, the problem is simply on us. It's not social media's problem if we fail to cope-up with reality. There are several books and articles that explore the fact that social media is triggering these psychological problems. Even for some time, I was also convinced that it was the case. I have considered social media to be the "main villain" for a long time.

However, the reality is not in everyone's life social media is the villain that leads to anxiety or depression. The evidence that everyone puts up to argue how social media inflicts mental problems does not have actual data or logic to back it. So, why is social media blamed?

Well, it is the most interesting part. Since the 2000s, social media usage has increased exponentially and it is a well-known fact. Similarly, the cases of depression, anxiety and other psychological issues have increased too in the new millennium. But that does not imply that social media is the big bad here. We are wrongly convicting it for something without having solid evidence.

Let me explain it clearly for you. Suppose, you went to four places for some purpose. One person was found to be murdered in all the places you went on the same day. So, obviously, the people will suspect you to have some connection with the murder since you have been in all the places where the murders were committed on the same day. But for you, it was just a coincidence and you had nothing to do with the incidents.

Nevertheless, to prove that you are innocent, it will take proper investigation and strong evidence. The same thing has happened with social media. It happens to have gained wide popularity in a time when the psychological problems are on the rise. So, it did not take much time for people to blame it for everything without looking for evidence seriously. The only way social media could have cleared its name was with the help of proper survey and investigation of the matter. But a survey of this caliber would have taken a great amount of time as well as money. So, most of the people did not bother.

Luckily, a group of researchers decided to look into the matter seriously. They kept track of some five hundred adolescents over a period of eight years to understand the effects of social media usage. The study revealed that social media has no connection with increasing mental health problems in society. Despite the results, no one highlighted the facts much since it was not appropriate for a spicy headline.

I came across the findings of this study in a hard-core science magazine and was really surprised myself. So, who is to blame for the increasing mental health issues then? This question was eating me up from the inside. Hence, I decided to look into the matter.

After conducting a lot of research myself, I came to the conclusion that our habits, socio-economic structure and our culture are to be blamed for all the problems.

The unstable global economic market, deficits, low availability of liquid cash in the hands of the people, unemployment, the corporate culture are indeed contributing to the increasing depression, anxiety and other mental health issues greatly. And there is no denying it. There are several pieces of evidence to support this conclusion of mine.

What other factors are at play? Well, you will be surprised to hear. Sleep deprivation is one of the major causes of mental health issues. And most of the people nowadays are sleep deprived. It may sound very shocking but it is true. Though you might say that you sleep 5 or 6 hours daily. But is it really true? Are you really getting all the sound sleep your body requires?

Our hectic schedule and habits have made us somewhat insomniac. Most of the people nowadays do not sleep well at night and that is causing half the problem.

When I learnt about the connection between sleep

deprivation and mental illness, I was shocked to my core. I was so scared that I changed my sleeping habits and tried my best to get a good night's sleep. And it helped! It made me much productive, happier and stress-free. So, sleeping is very important!

Finally, our desire to always hope for the best is also to be blamed for depression and anxiety. We often overlook the negative side of things. We always hope that everything will be good in the end.

But that is not the case in reality. Everything may not be good and hoping something like that prevents you from being rational and analytical. In the end, when our hopes do not get fulfilled, it fills us with regrets and dissatisfaction which in return gives rise to mental problems. So, there is no point on being positive all the times. Rather be rational, analyze the situation and every aspect of life and accept things as they stand. It will help in the end.

Social media may get blamed for everything. But it is not really the cause behind increasing mental health problems. Thus, know the causes and act on them. It is the only way to live a happy and healthy life.

So my suggestion, get to the roots of the problems, study the reasons and then come to the conclusion!

BALANCING
SOCIAL MEDIA
AND YOUR LIFE

8

SOCIAL MEDIA DETOXIFICATION: NO MORE FOMO

"Just as one goes on a fast or a body cleanse you owe it to yourselves to detox your mind, it will not be easy but easy never yielded lasting results."

— **Aysha Taryam**

The world of social media is full of glitter and attractions. With so much online content, gossip, gaming, shopping and discussion available on social media platforms, almost no one can overlook its allure. As a result, the more you get immersed in the world of social media, the more you get addicted to it.

The technology of social media is developing rapidly. In fact, the platforms are being made more intelligent than ever. Social media platforms can now actually understand what you like and dislike. So, they shape the contents featured in your feed in a way that you can remain entertained forever. As a result, the chances of getting addicted to social media are greater than ever.

As you log in to your profile, you will be able to see videos and posts that actually match your interests. This keeps you from getting bored with social media for a long time. It also modifies friend suggestions so that it only shows the people with whom your interests match. So you will never get tired of using it.

Even a few years back, it was easy to neglect social media and live your life without depending on it. However, as time passes and the technology improves to keep people bound to it, it has become a monster that consumes lives completely.

You might try to get out of this addiction but the attractions are so strong that it prompts you to log back in and enjoy the things that it offers. Though social media addiction is far different from any other type of addiction, it still consumes lives and detaches you from the reality surrounding you. You start living a life full of fantasies and neglect the ambitions and dreams you have.

Now you may ask: Why is it that you need to go through social media detoxification?

Have you heard about FOMO?

Yeah, it's very millennial of me! But the true fact is, I am very generation X.

However, the true meaning of FOMO or Fear Of Missing Out is associated with a huge percentage of social media users.

To be transparent with you, I was one of those individuals.

Giving constant updates appeared to be a mandatory duty.

When social media was non-existent, we never bothered to communicate if some random individual went on a luxury yacht trip. But now it's all in our feed.

Thus, if you missed any happening story going around anywhere in the world, it never bothered you. And so it would not result in FOMO.

There is absolutely no reason to attend a famous New Year's party just because you need to flaunt your happening life to the social media crowd. If you are comfortable being all alone on any occasion, then so be it!

FOMO will not only change you as an individual but you would certainly not enjoy doing something that you never preferred. And social media was meant to be fun, not a liability.

Nowadays, people are forgetting to become a person of their own; rather, they are valuing the opinions of others more than their own. Most important, social media is also spreading hatred. People judge each other too quickly, making fun of others and ultimately hurting each other.

Social media is also spreading violence in terms of race, religion and everything that seems really disgraceful in this modern day. People are making hate posts, promoting intolerance and starting social unrest on a mass scale. So you can say that going through social media detoxification seems to be the ideal choice in the present day.

If you can truly go through the process of social media detoxification, it will actually help you feel good about yourself by boosting your self-confidence. You will no longer have to depend on the opinions of other people.

Plus, it will help you focus your mind and energy on the more important things in life without wasting a lot of time on social media platforms. Above all, the detoxification process will help you form real-life connections rather than investing in phony and plastic ones.

But how will you conduct the social media detoxification process?

It is not at all easy as it may sound. The attractions of social media platforms are so great that it will actually require you to use every bit of your mental strength to get rid of the addiction. So, you will have to be very strict about it and you will need to have complete control over yourself. If you cannot hold on to your strength of character then you will never be able to complete the detoxification process.

First of all, you need to understand the nature of social media addiction. Social media addiction is a mental addiction rather than a substance addiction.

When you use social media, it promotes the secretion of dopamine that provides you with instant gratification as well as happiness. Thus, you can obviously understand that social media detoxification has to be done in a much different way than detoxifying your body of any drug.

The detoxification process can last as long as you can choose it to be. But you must be disconnected from social media platforms for at least 100 days in order to make it successful.

Well, there is nothing to worry about. Let me walk you through the process as clearly as possible so that you completely detox your mind against social media addiction and make your life much happier.

Get out of the trap of social media:

"It's so funny how social media was just this fun thing, and now it's this monster that consumes so many millennial lives," the famous American actor **Cazzie David** accurately said this.

I said to my elder daughter, "Better not become obsessed with selfies. It might turn out to be dangerous, you know."

And the laughter that I got in return didn't please me at all.

It was the father in me that acted out of concern after I came across a story of a 19-year-old kid named Danny Bowman.

A perfect millennial kid who loved clicking selfies and being on social media, he wanted to always post picture-perfect selfies. Bowman's case was so extreme that he had spent almost 10 hours a day on his iPhone. And when he failed in perfecting the art of clicking a selfie, he tried to commit suicide. Chills!

This kid was so obsessed with the whole social media life that he dropped out of school, put his health at risk and even lost his friends. What else could have gone wrong?

Being a father, this did cause me a lot of stress but later I realized that it's better to tell my concerns to my daughter rather than just forcing her to stop doing it.

But a detoxification process must be imposed at least once every 3 months to keep the habit under control.

Well, the very first thing that you can do to successfully achieve social media detoxification is to get rid of the social media itself. What do I mean by that? Well, the meaning is very simple: you will have to lose all your connections to social media as early as possible.

Wait, wait! No reason to panic. I mean just go through a simple cleansing process.

Well, deactivating all your social media profiles is not a suggestion but rather a stupidity. What's life without some sort of entertainment?

Start by removing unwanted and negative human beings from your account. The more you keep unnecessary and negative people, the more you will feel the necessity to listen to the opinion of others. Simply do it!

Next, focus your energy on other day-to-day activities. Trade the extra time you spend on social media for any activity that will have some positive impact. And boom! Now you can minimize your activity time on social media and concentrate on real-life goals.

If that doesn't work, you can simply switch to the easiest solution. That's uninstalling!

Whenever needed, uninstall the social media apps from your phone and take a break. You can just get back to it anytime.

However, the most important point is, never install or surf through any social media platform on the laptop or PC you use for work. It is a major distraction. Follow this one strict rule and your workspace productivity will increase.

Above all, I suggest you block the links of social media platforms in your browsers. Then you can stay true to yourself and go through the detoxification process with utmost efficiency.

As I have already said, the very first step towards social media detoxification is to get rid of the trappings of social media. So, the steps listed above will help you do it with ease.

However, the process of social media detoxification is not complete yet. The hardest part is to stick to the choice you have made by following the steps above. Well, let me help you do it.

Focus on real-life activities and replace social media with other activities:

Obviously, this has to be the most crucial thing to do when it comes to social media detoxification. The hardest thing about social media detoxification is to complete it. Uninstalling social media apps or deactivating profiles is easy to do. However, the real challenge comes when you actually need to live by the choice you have made to go through the detoxification process. Let me tell you an easy way to do it.

The best thing that you can do is to replace social media with some other activity. Why do you need to do that? Well, if you cannot find something that makes you feel good just like social media does, then you will never be able to get rid of it fully.

You can invest your time in hobbies, take up exercising, go on trips, read books and engage with others in real life in order to get rid of your social media dependency. Once you are able to replace the need for social media with something else then you will be able to completely detox yourself without trying to get back to it.

I remember when my social media addiction almost snatched all my free time from me. Every social media user knows that this addiction is no less than alcohol or smoking addiction.

A year back I was trying to take up social media detoxification in order to cleanse my mind and focus on more important things in life.

So, I started in the way I suggested previously. I deactivated all my profiles. Deleted all the apps from my mobile phone and completely removed every bit of connection I had with social media.

However, the storm was yet to come. For the first few days, everything went very smoothly. I didn't feel any urge to use social media. But it changed suddenly! As the days passed by, I was really getting weary of the detoxification process. And I was finding ways to break my promise to not use social media.

I tried to stick firmly to my rules but it was just like the way you crave fast foods during your diet.

Though I knew what I was doing was not right, still, the attraction was too strong to ignore. When I was on the verge of giving in, I surrendered to my wife for help.

She patiently heard everything that I was experiencing and understood my problems.

"It is not easy to give up an addiction. You will have to be patient and strong," she said after listening to me.

"Yes, I know. But how? How will I do it? How will I ignore the attractions?" I asked.

"Well, why don't you replace social media with something else?" she said.

"What do you mean?" I asked being a little confused about what she was suggesting.

"Social media makes you feel good and happy. Doesn't it? That is exactly why you use it. So, why don't you find an activity that recreates the same feelings? It will help you to overlook the lurings of social media and focus in your life in a much better way," she replied.

I readily understood what she was suggesting and thanked God for giving me such an intelligent life partner.

Immediately, I decided to join a dance class as I was always psyched about learning how to dance. Within a few days, it completely made me forget social media. And once again I was my confident self without having to depend on a digital platform to feel good about myself.

Here's a lesser known fact about me: I channeled that energy into focusing on my fitness classes as well. It not only helped me physically but I was satisfied mentally.

"I am pain-stricken to say, that today's so-called modern humans are all like the dogs in Pavlov's experiment. Pavlov used a bell to manipulate the mind of his dogs, and today, social media platforms are using people's own beloved smartphones to manipulate them." — **Abhijit Naskar**, a famous neuroscientist of the modern age, said this in one of his lectures. And he absolutely speaks the truth.

So, committing to social media detoxification has become much more important than ever in order to live your life freely without being manipulated by social media.

9

CONTROL YOUR ADDICTION TO START WINNING IN LIFE

"The more social media we have, the more we think we're connecting, yet we are really disconnecting from each other."

— JR

Last night, while I was reading one of the books by my favorite author, I was hit with a light of wisdom. How much did I miss feeling connected to my books? The smell and essence of the crisp paper, it's just blissful. Now it astounds me how foolish I was to trade my old habits for the sake of spending time on social media.

A normal morning now usually doesn't start with you reading the morning newspaper, but with receiving endless notifications as soon as you turn on the internet. A Sunday midday nap is now replaced with sharing memes on Facebook or retweeting any tweet. Does that sound relatable?

Sometimes we forget that to share memories, you need to create memories. And it can only happen if you communicate, venture to places, explore your creative side and so on. In short, you need to create quality content for sharing content and making an impression on others.

Well, you can argue with yourself and justify your addiction but what about people who just unknowingly get involved in all your social media games?

Last year, I was in an international meeting for entrepreneurs. It was a high-esteem event and had certain strict codes that needed to be maintained. One such code was to keep everyone's phone away in a locker while the event was being held. So there was no livestreaming or updates after we entered the event space.

Similarly, not all the people at events and parties want to put themselves out in the world, and livestreaming them without having their consent will do no good. Or the host may feel that posting anything related to the party is a breach of privacy but hesitate to do anything about it.

Hence, once entrapped in social media addiction, you tend to forget the basic manners of asking for consent from others before posting about them on any social platforms. This uncontrolled use may make you do many things that may not be appreciated by all.

However, you may ask if it is wrong to capture photos of your graduation day or during birthday parties and post them? Of course not! In fact, framing these moments has always been common among individuals. Even my dad clicked photographs whenever we were on a vacation or something special happened. But remember, social media was not a thing back in the 1900s. So the matter of controlling social media addiction never was a concern.

Well, in this whole controlled usage process, we have forgotten to take a certain section of our society into consideration. And that is our children. Children and young adults are one of the most affected groups.

So, how can we stop them from getting sucked into social media addiction? How can we fix it?

I have the answer!

Back in 2014, a piece of heart-wrenching news gave me some sleepless nights. Being a father of three daughters, I couldn't help but think about my their safety. News broke that an Indian army official's daughter from Gorakhpur chose to take her life when her mother scolded her for overusing Facebook. She locked herself up in her room soon after her mom scolded her, and the next morning she was found hanging from the ceiling.

Clearly, her mother tried to help her with her social media addiction but it seems she refused to have a life without social media.

So, now you can see why parents need to find a solution to keep children away from overuse of social media.

After thinking and studying parenting books, I figured out that nothing is better than the good old method of "talking." No more grounding them for not going by the rules, just have a heart-to-heart conversation. Neither scold them nor use any harsh words, just simply make them understand the advantages and disadvantages of social media and let them decide for themselves when they are old enough. Now it will be up to them if they want an unhappy life ruined by social media addiction or a happy life with controlled use of social media.

You, as a parent, will know exactly how your child will react and in what circumstances. So, formulate a conversation that can bring no harm to your child and yet prevent social media addiction.

The plan that I chose was a conversation over a daddy-daughter date. And that really worked!

Now let's go back to adult addiction and its relation to social media.

Don't you think a spontaneous coffee date will give you more happiness than spending your days checking on the like and love reacts you have got on your photo?

There are some things that are better done in real life than on social media. Think, how would you feel if you were paid in reacts, shares and retweets for the work you do in your workspace? Would you appreciate it?

I am pretty sure that the answer is NO as it would be of no value in real life. So now imagine how vague a conversation with your long-lost high school friend would be if done only on social media platforms.

So is it right? Is it right to depend on social media to make yourself feel special?

No, it is not.

Just as social media platforms are bringing people together and making friendship circles stronger, they also have given rise to trash talking. Some love to chitter and chatter while others just love to be all negative and bring down people.

Well, even this is a sort of addiction. The satisfaction that some gain from being shady and mean to others has escalated pretty quickly in this age of social media. So now you can classify social media addiction in a broader way. It's up to you what activities and what sort of happiness you derive out of social media. But the addiction is serious.

In fact, it is one of the most pressing concerns of modern life. More than any other drug, social media addiction destroys the lives of people.

"As far as self-confidence goes, so much of social media is about approval, getting likes, comparing our lives to others' - meanwhile, confidence is an inside job: it's about how you feel about yourself regardless of what anyone else does or thinks. It's a knowing that you're human, you're flawed, and you're awesome in your own way." — **Jen Sincero**, a famous American author, said this in one of her interviews. And it beautifully summarizes everything that I have been trying to say so far.

Now, the question is how do you get out of the grasp of social media and take the reins of your life in your own hands?

Well, the answer to it is actually very simple. Detox, or if that fails, deactivate your social media accounts and you will be able to achieve unprecedented success in your life.

Of course, deactivating your accounts and living by this choice is not easy. It takes a lot of self-control and strength of character to resist the lure of social media. But once you can do it, it will help you achieve great things in your life.

In this chapter, I will help you understand how you can deactivate your social media profiles and start winning in your life. I will provide you with tips and real-life examples to help you understand the concepts to apply in your own life.

Social media deactivation: Make real-life connection with others:

Of course, social media was developed to help people connect with each other. But is it performing in the way that it was envisaged? No, it is not! We are no longer connecting with others through social media rather we are getting disconnected from our loved ones due to our overuse of social media.

This common example will help you understand what I am trying to say. Suppose, you have six hundred friends in your Facebook account and two hundred followers in your Instagram.

But how many of these people do you actually talk to or know in real life? They like or leave a comment on your pictures or posts and you do the same. So, can you say that you are connected with them? No, you cannot.

On the contrary, there might be several people you knew or were good friends with back in your high school or college days with whom you are no longer connected. And that is a problem that social media has created. All of us are living under a falsehood.

But you can change it. You have the power to bring about a change to the situation as well as in your life. You can again be connected with people you hold dear and actually be happy without the need for social media. All you need to do is just deactivate your social media profiles and live your life to the fullest.

Being an entrepreneur, I have my own struggles and overcoming the addiction of social media is one of those. I had to have several aha! moments before I took complete control of my addiction.

This incident happened a year back. I really realized the importance of deactivating social media and how it helps in winning in life.

Even though I have previously gone through social media detoxification (a story that I shared with you in the previous chapter), I still felt oddly connected to it.

I would always find myself surfing through my social media profiles and posting regular updates.

Though I was not an avid user, still it felt very satisfying. I would post updates about every little thing and try to prove to the world how perfect my life was. I would get tons of praise from my followers and other people. But in reality, my life was far from being perfect.

In reality, my closest ones - my wife and children - were all addicted to social media like I was. We were all trapped in the pretentious web of social media and we did not know how to get rid of it.

Before social media became a thing, my children would come running to give me a hug when I would come back from work. My wife would kiss me goodnight while going to sleep. She would bring a glass of water every time I returned home all tired and ask me how my day was. My life was perfect and I was truly a happy man.

But then social media happened!

Everything changed so fast without us even noticing. My children were no longer greeting me with a warm hug upon returning home. I would find them sitting on the couch or in their rooms with their mobiles in their hands.

My wife would no longer kiss me goodnight since we both used to go to sleep once we got tired of using social media. She stopped asking me how my day was since she was also busy with Instagram, Snapchat or Facebook. Things were the same on my part too. I was no longer giving them the time that I used to. I was also busy with my phone.

But strangely none of us ever felt the difference. We never

noticed that so much had changed in our happy little family. Until one day!

One day we were all sitting at the dining table eating our dinner. I was eating my food while watching a video about the problems that social media has given rise to on Facebook. It was talking about the ways social media has disconnected us from our loved ones.

Suddenly, I found my plate empty and I looked up to get a piece of bread from the bowl. It was the exact moment when I realized that the same thing was happening to me and my family. I saw everyone else was glued to their mobile phones like me while eating their dinner.

I felt remorseful. I did not know what to do. It suddenly hit me hard and made me realize how disconnected I had become from the people I love most in my life.

I did not say anything and finished dining. After dinner, I talked with my wife about it. She was freaked out too upon realizing what social media had turned us into. So, we decided to do something about it.

We deactivated our social media profiles and started to live our lives once again as we used to. Within a few days, the scenario changed completely. I was once again being greeted at the door by my children. I was once again being handed that glass of water and asked how my day was. And our connections were stronger than ever.

I won't say that using social media is a bad thing. But the usage needs to be controlled or in extreme cases, cut off altogether. So, if you really want to connect with the people in your life without having to live the life that social media has created, then deactivate it. You will win things in your life which you never thought possible.

"Social media, unfortunately, just makes it a lot easier to be jealous. It sets up false expectations of reality, so it's really easy to look at someone else's life online and assume that they have everything going great for them and that their life is perfect." — Comedian **Francesca Ramsey** said this on a talk show and it serves as a beautiful summary to everything that I have said.

Life goals or social media? One needs to be sacrificed:

The answer is very obvious. Social media does waste a lot of our time. You spend hours on social media surfing through your feed and checking on what others are doing.

Imagine a future with no dreams achieved, no real friends and family to support you and no money to live on. But only social media accounts to make you feel their virtual presence.

Do you want such a life for yourself? I am not saying that your life will end up this way but there is a chance that you may wander around aimless and with unfulfilled goals if you fail to find a balance between social media and real life.

Social media can be lucrative if you know the right ways to cash in on it. And it will be fun until it starts controlling you and not the opposite.

Truth be told, life will look bleak if goals are not achieved and then social media accounts will bring no happiness in your life.

So, do not waste time on unnecessary things on social media. Reduce the hours you spend on it instead! Invest that time in the things you love to do. You will feel the difference soon enough. You will feel that everything you set your eyes on can be achieved. You will regain that confidence in yourself.

Social media is nothing but a beautiful lie. Don't get trapped by it. Live your life and I guarantee you victory.

10

HOW TO GET RID OF SOCIAL MEDIA ADDICTION AND SPEND TIME WITH CLOSE ONES IN REAL LIFE

"Social media sites create an illusion of connectivity."

— Malay Shah

When social media was just gaining popularity, we still knew what privacy was. Then the addiction specifically hit teens and young adults in the early stages of its growth. Now, there is hardly any individual that is unaware of the term "SOCIAL MEDIA." The growth was predictable but the thing that was unpredictable was the loss of privacy.

Yes! The term privacy had a meaning before but now it seems to have gotten lost in the digital age.

Before the rise of social media, we knew that it was time to sleep when hallucinations started taking us over. But now we can't tear ourselves away from social media and we lose track of bedtime. I remember seeing my friends drawing sketches when they didn't feel sleepy. And they would bring the masterpieces they created to school. But now sleepless nights mean surfing through social media. Even midnight talks have lost importance.

Sharing personal achievements, birthday photos, travel pictures and any other photos as well as updates will bother no one. But when your family and closest friends, whom you have known forever, get to know about your happy or sad moments through social media, that's where you break the rule. And I know exactly how deep it hurts.

Last year, my cousin and his wife were expecting a child. And guess how we, his family, came to know about it? Of course, through social media. It seemed like we were the sheep of the herd who are generalized despite being someone of utmost importance in their life.

So, how is it bringing people closer?

Now, you can obviously ask how it distances you from the real world and people dear to you. Well, let me give you an example to help you understand the problem. Suppose, you have twelve hundred friends in your Facebook profile. Now, for a moment, I ask you to be honest with yourself.

Well, if you ask yourself honestly then you will find that you do not even know 90 percent of the people that are connected with you in your Facebook profile. Even if you are connected with a lot of people on social media, you have no idea about the existence of most of these people, which in turn makes such connections pointless. And it does distance you from the people that matter in your life and the reality of life itself.

Now, you may not only start getting detached from your loved ones but sometimes even yourself. With time, life experiences may change us to someone else. However, what if it's not the experiences but social media addiction that's turning you into someone that you were never in reality?

You may be aware of the term cyber-bullying. It usually refers to situations where an individual or a group of individuals target and bully someone on a social media platform. Sometimes, this bullying may even lead to situations where the victim gives up life as it becomes too much to bear.

So, now let's just focus on yourself. Try to remember, have you ever commented something unrelated and mean on a complete stranger's post? If so, then you are doing a crime; you are cyber-bullying. Knowingly or unknowingly, you are committing a crime that is punishable.

But most importantly, you are losing yourself. Yes, you are distancing yourself from the real you and that's the biggest flaw of social media addiction.

Often there are cases where the person of interest is seen wearing a virtual mask.

In reality, the bully might be a fun-loving person but in the social media world, he or she loves to taunt and harass people. Sometimes it's classified as the nature of the individual but most of the time, it's just a mask that the person wears to look cool among friends.

Social media often indirectly manipulates users to portray a certain character or nature that's completely different from our real nature in order to earn appreciation and acceptance. And sometimes in the process of gaining appreciation, we tend to step into something that's absolutely not justifiable or acceptable to the world.

Here is where we not only get disconnected from the people in our life but also SELF. And losing SELF to social media is the biggest defeat you can witness in your lifetime. So before trying to reconnect yourself with the individuals whom you lost, find a connection to your true self.

That's the first step towards fixing your relationship with others.

How can someone put trust in an individual who doesn't feel or sound to be himself or herself?

Once you are done with the self-searching, it's time to reinstate the relationship with your friends and family.

Now take for example the reason behind going on vacation. We want to escape the humdrum of daily life and look forward to spending worry-free time with our near and dear ones. Similarly, we can take some time out from the chaos of the social media world and stop worrying about likes, shares retweets for some time. So, let's look into this reason for convincing yourself to take a social media break!

"We and others have done a bunch of work to show that if

your real friends online say or do something, it affects you. But if your acquaintances online say or do something, it does not. People, on average, have about 106 Facebook friends, but only five or six real friends." — **Nicholas A. Christakis**, sociologist and physician, actually speaks the truth and wonderfully summarizes everything that I have been trying to say so far.

So, let us not waste time and dive into the depth of the concepts.

What to do? How to be active in real life? Take a deep breath and let's start it today:

Obviously, this is the foremost thing that you can do in this aspect. As I have said before, social media entraps you in a world of illusion. You think that you are famous among others; you have a lot of people in your life. However, the reality is completely different.

In reality, you get distant from the people you love without even noticing. You think that you do not have time to spend with others due to your busy schedule. Nonetheless, if you stop wasting countless hours you spend on social media to actually spend some time with your close ones, then you will actually be able to be happy in life without having to live a lie.

Well, my life is no different. This happened a year back. As I have pointed out over the course of this book, I was addicted to social media at one point of my life and it is one of the incidents from that time that actually motivated me to get out of my social media addiction. This incident revolved around one of the closest people in my life, my cousin.

I have a cousin named Kamran. Though we were cousins, we had grown up as siblings and we had always been very close to each other.

He was the person that I could always rely on. We used to spend time together and go on our little adventures. He was always my partner in crime.

Whether skipping classes to watch a movie or trying a cigarette for the first time, we always used to do everything together. We were actually inseparable.

He knew all my secrets and I knew his. If there was one person who always had my back, it was him. But things changed after we finished college. I started my own business and he went to get an MBA degree then got placed in a multinational company. We no longer had much time to hang out with each other. However, we used to meet and go on trips whenever we could.

Well, that also stopped after a while. Of course, social media had a great role to play in this. I used to like and comment on his posts or pictures on social media. Somewhere in my mind I was convinced that I was strongly connected to him through all this. So, I never felt the urge to meet with my cousin even though he asked me several times to make plans.

The illusion faded away!

One day I saw that Kamran had updated a life event on Facebook. He was promoted to the position of CEO of his company. It was great news but I felt kind of sad at the same time. I still remembered the time when he called me with all the excitement when he got his job. But today, he did not even bother to inform me of such great news. I was happy for him and somewhat heartbroken at the same time.

I asked myself, "Where did I go wrong? Why did we suddenly become so distant from each other?"

I could not figure out anything. Suddenly, my eyes went to the Facebook logo.

And I felt foolish. I chose social media over everything. I remembered how Kamran would ask me to make plans and want to hang out. But I never bothered to heed to his requests or even call him to talk. I was happy knowing that I was connected with him through social media.

I realized the mistake I had made. So, I did not waste time. I deactivated my social media accounts and picked up my phone to call Kamran.

I congratulated him on his achievement and apologized for neglecting his requests for so long. We had a nice heart-to-heart conversation and we planned to go on a trip together.

Everything was back to normal once again. I was again connected with one of the closest people in my life.

So, you can obviously understand how important it is to actually spend time with the people who are close to you. Cut down on or even get rid of social media. Spend as much time as you can with the people you love. That is the way to live a happy life.

Real life problems need real-life solutions:

Let's start the detoxification process by switching off our notifications. Yes, you heard it right! Scroll down and tap on the settings of the individual apps and mute the notifications so that you don't get distracted every time. But one of the most harmful things is staring at bright screens and surfing through social media before you finally take your eyes off the screen. As per research, it minimizes the generation of melatonin, popularly known as the sleep hormone.

As a matter of fact, it is not surprising if you lose sleep. Well, you can solve your problem by switching to black-and-white display. Too much exposure to light, especially during dark hours, will not benefit you. Simply go from colored phone settings to black-and-white ones.

Don't know how to activate it? Come on! If you belong to the tech-savvy generation, you definitely know how to do it. And if not, do a Google search. Google has the answer to everything. But if you have no clue about that as well? Then just seek help from friends or family. It won't take much time to learn.

Also, turn the night mode on; it will keep you away from spending unwanted time on social media.

Moreover, there are also certain apps that will help you to limit your social media activities. One such app is the Forest app. You can just enter the desired time, say 30 minutes. During this period of time, you are not allowed to do any activity. And if you perform any activity on your phone during that given time, the tree growing on the phone will instantly die. So, it is an interactive app.

Plus, traveling always soothes the soul and helps clear your mind. But what most people do not know is that traveling also helps you connect with people on a different level.

If you travel with someone or go on vacations together, you get a good amount of time to spend together. As a result, you get to know the person in a much better way. The beautiful ambience can prompt hearty conversations which can further strengthen your bond.

This is something that you will never be able to achieve through social media. Commenting on or reacting to someone's posts does not help you strengthen the bond or know the person in a better way. It only distances you from the truth.

So, do not waste your time on social media. Go on vacations with people you love, try to spend as much time as you can with them. This will help you to not only mature as a person but also live a happy life.

"Social media has given us this idea that we should all have a posse of friends when in reality, if we have one or two really good friends, we are lucky." — **Brené Brown**, the popular American author, extraordinarily describes the irony of social media.

CONCLUSION

Now that you are clear about the GOOD, the BAD, and the UGLY of social media, here is a quick summary of how to make it beneficial for you in all ways. Note the points and learn to control your use of social media as well as make it work on your own terms.

Tips to come out as a winner in this social media addiction game:

- Social media is a great platform for marketing, instilling social awareness and communicating with people. Make the most of it to benefit yourself and your work.
- The Golden Rule is to practice self-control and become disciplined. Work on resisting your urge to stay connected on social media always.
- Create a social media menu per your own requirements. Devise rules that that will satisfy your ego, and that you will be able to stand by.
- Install apps that will aid you in having full control over your addiction.
- Set up a penalty jar where you drop a certain amount

every time you fail to abide by the rules. Donate the money for a good cause or charity.

- Maintain a balance between social media life and real life. Real-life activities are an essential part of life. Do not detach yourself from real-life activities for the sake of social media.
- Focus on work and do not let social media distract you in your professional area.
- If everything above fails, then the final option is uninstalling the apps or seeking the help of professionals, or both. This is the ultimate solution and you should go for it only if things have really gotten out of hand.

The idea of social media is totally different among individuals. It's fun, it's engaging, it's interactive, but it can also be scary, upsetting—and addictive. The underlying truth is that social media isn't the real reason for the turmoil in your life. Rather, it's your lack of self-control. So, try to look for the positives in social media and use this book to help bring you a successful, prosperous, and tension-free life.